finishing
WELL

Learning to LIVE
Through Terminal Illness

finishing
WELL

Learning to LIVE
Through Terminal Illness

by John Eaves

KINGSLEY BOOKS, INC.
NASHVILLE, TENNESSEE

FINISHING WELL

Copyright © 2007 Kay Eaves

All rights reserved. Written permission must be secured from
the publisher to use or reproduce any part of this book except
for brief quotations in critical reviews and articles.

Published in Nashville, Tennessee, by Kingsley Books, Inc.,
P.O. Box 121584, Nashville, Tennessee 37212.

All Scripture quotations, unless otherwise noted, are taken
from The Holy Bible, New International Version (NIV).
Copyright © 1973, 1978, 1984. International Bible Society.
Used by permission of Zondervan Bible Publishers.

Scripture quotations noted MSG are taken from The Message,
copyright © 1993. Used by permission of NavPress Publishing
Group.

Library of Congress Cataloging-in-Publication Data
on file
ISBN-10: 1-58334-444-6
ISBN-13: 978-1-58334-444-6

Printed in the United States of America
07 08 09 10 11 XXX 9 8 7 6 5 4 3 2 1

Contents

And what more shall I say? I do not have time to tell about Gideon, Barak, Samson, Jephthah, David, Samuel and the prophets, who through faith conquered kingdoms, administered justice, and gained what was promised; who shut the mouths of lions, quenched the fury of the flames, and escaped the edge of the sword; whose weakness was turned to strength; and who became powerful in battle and routed foreign armies. Women received back their dead, raised to life again. Others were tortured and refused to be released, so that they might gain a better resurrection. Some faced jeers and flogging, while still others were chained and put in prison. They were stoned; they were sawed in two; they were put to death by the sword. They went about in sheepskins and goatskins, destitute, persecuted and mistreated—the world was not worthy of them. They wandered in deserts and mountains, and in caves and holes in the ground.

*These were all commended for their faith, yet
none of them received what had been promised.
God had planned something better for us so that
only together with us would they be made perfect.*

*Therefore, since we are surrounded by
such a great cloud of witnesses, let us throw off
everything that hinders and the sin that so easily
entangles, and let us run with perseverance
the race marked out for us. Let us fix our eyes
on Jesus, the author and perfecter of our faith,
who for the joy set before him endured the cross,
scorning its shame, and sat down at the right
hand of the throne of God. Consider him who
endured such opposition from sinful men, so that
you will not grow weary and lose heart.*

Hebrews 11:32–12:3

Introduction

When my friend John Eaves learned he had colon cancer, he called me. He understood the course set before him and purposed to run it well. In reality, though, he had lived those last months exactly the way he lived the previous years. Long before a doctor delivered bad health news, John had learned to live by faith. Feelings and circumstances would not govern his life. Although cancer presented a new hurdle, he regrouped and kept running. His race reminds me of the passage in Hebrews 12:1–2.

Therefore, since we are surrounded by such a great cloud of witnesses, let us throw off everything that hinders and the sin that so easily entangles, and let us run with perseverance the race marked out for us. Let us fix our eyes on Jesus, the author and perfecter of our faith, who for the joy set before him endured the cross, scorning its shame, and sat down at the right hand of the throne of God.

Throughout his life, John focused on Jesus and ran the race of faith. Nothing distracted him; nothing stopped him. He rebuffed any suggestion that his manner of living was anything special. To him, his life of faith was normal for a Christian. John taught others as he lived. He didn't talk about faith; he simply believed God.

Some time after John died, I dreamed I was standing in a hallway. I turned and saw John coming down a staircase. Even in my dream I knew he was dead, but I was thrilled to see him. He walked straight toward me, pointed at me, and asked, "Why don't you believe?"

I was stunned. Behind John was a group of young men I did not know. They followed him into an adjoining room and formed a semi-circle behind him. I followed them into the room. Confused and stinging from his blunt question, I looked at John and asked, "Who are they?" John replied simply, "They are here for you."

And then I woke up. I puzzled over the dream's meaning but sensed God would use it powerfully in my life. For some reason, God was using my friend to challenge me to a higher level of faith.

The next night, I lay in bed pondering that dream and thinking about John. The Lord reminded me of a song I had written more than twenty years before, called "The Runner's Song." The words ran through my mind:

A lone runner ran down a dusty road;
his body ached from the weight of his load.
Dreams of the finish line seemed to explode
for the race was far too long.

"I can run no more," he said with a cry.
But just at that moment a man ran by.
He matched the pace of the runner's stride
and began to sing this song.

"Run, keep on running, you'll finish the race.
Fix your eyes on me and then I'll set the pace.
Cast off anything that will hinder you.
Run . . . for your race is almost through."

And with those words the man pulled ahead.
The runner thought of the words he'd said.
But soon his gaze was drawn instead
to the body of the man.

For his feet were maimed from an awful blow;
his hands were marred by a wound long ago.
With each stride the pain would show,
but the man still sang this song.

"Run, keep on running, you'll finish the race.
Fix your eyes on me and then I'll set the pace.
Cast off anything that will hinder you.
Run . . . for your race is almost through."

They topped a hill and there below
stood a coliseum grand.
The greatest runners of all time
were seated in the stands.

As they entered in the crowd began
to urge them round the field.
In the song they sang the man's name ran
. . . a mystery revealed.

"Run, keep on running, you'll finish the race.
Fix your eyes on me and then I'll set the pace.
Cast off anything that will hinder you.
Run . . . for your race is almost through."

Jesus ran so we follow Him.
We compete as those who know we'll win.
The prize awaits God's champions—
the faithful who'll endure.

With each step He's by our side;
those who've come before look on in pride.
We'll end our course and come inside
to join The Runner's Song.

Then I understood my dream. My
friend was in the stands of faithful witnesses
exhorting me to run hard and finish well. John

had joined the stands to sing "The Runner's Song."

The key to "finishing well" is to "live well." This is John Eaves's legacy: John finished well. This was his goal. He achieved that goal.

What this little book cannot tell is the larger story of John's life. To understand how John "finished well," you must know how he "lived well." The final lap of John's life was not a sprinter's burst fueled by adrenaline; it was the final leg in a marathon of faith.

John Kramp

Chapter One
Step by Step
by Sam House

John Eaves learned to walk in faith, no matter the circumstances.

A long the journey of life we all face hurdles, but what happens when the path we're on takes us in an unexpected direction? For John Eaves, the answer was to walk in faith. Every step of the way. Even in the face of cancer.

For eighteen months, John had been living in New York City, fulfilling a lifelong dream. It didn't look exactly as he or his wife, Kay, thought it would, though. John directed a ministry to internationals in Manhattan and

commuted to Nashville every month, while Kay stayed with their family and ministry in Tennessee.

"When we got married, we gave ourselves to the Lord to follow in whatever direction He led. In a lifetime of being sensitive [to God], we had seen and been in a lot of situations that surprised us," Kay says.

However, the announcement that John had stage 4 colon cancer with just months to live hit them like a ton of bricks. But after the initial shock, John decided to fully live each moment he had left. He wrote in a letter to friends and family: "I am praying that the days God gives will be some of the most meaningful in my life. I am not running to the sidelines. I am headed toward the center of the field."

A New York Dream From the
beginning of their life together, John and Kay committed to walk wherever God directed.

Both felt called to international missions while in college in Bowling Green, Kentucky, where they met and married. Soon after, God directed their steps to places like the Philippines and Uganda. Yet together they came to realize God wanted them to serve internationals living in the United States. So they began in 1980 by reaching out to international students and scholars attending Harvard and the Massachusetts Institute of Technology.

"Our dream for the last twenty years," Kay says, "had been to go to New York City"—an international crossroad. But God led them first to Nashville, Tennessee, where they became involved with InterFACE (International Friendship Activities and Cultural Exchange) Ministries, a mission with about fifty staff members across the United States that serves international students as well as immigrants and refugees. Together, John and Kay spent years building a team of more than one thousand community volunteers from thirty-eight local churches.

Their ministry with InterFACE flourished, and their sons—Jesse, Joshua, and Matthew—grew up in an atmosphere of sharing God's love by meeting the needs of people in practical ways.

Still, John and Kay never forgot their dream to serve internationals in New York City. The long-awaited opportunity finally presented itself when John was asked to direct Hephzibah House, a ministry to internationals similar to InterFACE.

Jesse had finished college, and Joshua was graduating, but until Matthew finished high school, the Eaves felt certain God was directing Kay to remain in Nashville while John moved to Manhattan. Kay and a very capable board of advisors would keep the Nashville ministry strong while, in New York City, John would train and mentor the next generation of ministers to internationals. Though this was the beginning of a dream come true, their excitement was tempered with an awareness that they would live apart for a time.

The couple put their trust in God and took a bold step of faith to divide their family between two cities. John summed up those days as "crazy but filled with purpose."

A Change of Plan

Fifteen months after arriving in New York City, John began to experience recurring abdominal pains. Further tests revealed a polyp. Surgery to remove the polyp revealed colon cancer.

"In almost a moment, God showed us great plans were not going to happen," Kay says. "I think a lifetime of trying to adjust our plans and dreams to God's direction prepared us. But [John's cancer] was still a shock."

As April 2003 came to a close, John returned to Nashville. Additional tests showed the cancer had spread to his lymph nodes and liver.

"Dad, why don't you just quit going to this doctor?" Matthew had asked. "Every time you go, they just give you bad news!"

John chuckled at his son's advice but responded, "Life is an incredible adventure of faith." He also considered how the Apostle Paul advanced toward his destiny. John's observation was simple: "Paul never gave up on life . . . I want to be like that."

A Life Shared While in New York City, John had poured his life into the

multinational staff at
Hephzibah House.
Wilbert Latuce, a
Haitian, quickly became
John's right arm and
served as a Bible study
teacher and leader in
conversational English
programs. When Eri

Inoue, a native of Japan, came to Hephzibah
House as an intern, she had been a Christian
for less than two years. As she grew in her
faith, she began to teach English as a second
language and to lead a popular book club
for international women. They also saw God
open doors at Columbia University.

As John joined his family in Nashville,
Wilbert and Eri found themselves leading the
mission on their own.

"I saw that God had already been at work
raising up the next generation of leaders in
Wilbert and Eri," John said. "It wasn't what
God was doing in me or what I was teaching

them . . . Mentoring is a life shared." John continued, "God literally raised up the next generation and put them in my life to share what He would do next in us.

"What we anticipated, as opposed to what actually happened, just proves that God was subtly at work in the small things to prepare for the huge things."

One Life's Impact John's one life
has impacted many. "A woman in the English class—influenced by the news that John was

facing death—told me that her mother had died of cancer several years ago," Eri says. "Now she wanted to know about God and the reason for living. She was encouraged to hear about John's response to the discovery of cancer."

"The universal paradigm," Wilbert says, "is that bad things happen to bad people and good things happen to good people, so a lot of people, not just internationals, had questions . . . That opens the door to tell people that it is not about us. It is about God's love for us."

Part of a Bigger Plan John's

family had to accept the fact that the destination they had felt led to was put into others' hands, at least for a time. They were also aware that many others were observing how they handled the upheaval in their lives.

"We have all become bolder in our faiths," Kay says. "A dying man can say anything he wants. His boldness has given us courage as a family—both to face this time and to share its meaning with others. It's not an easy thing for us to give thanks to God for John's life and also give thanks for what he is going through now.

"It's not about us, though," Kay continues. "We are part of a bigger plan . . . to show God's love to the whole world."

John said God had particularly brought Hebrews 11:32–12:3 to his mind. "This is one of the most realistic views of life in Scripture. When the list of godly men and women is given, the summary is that all of these were

commended for their faith. Some experienced miracles; others went through trials and hardship; and some even lost their lives. Yet all circumstances were opportunities to witness for God."

The Right Question

That Scripture fits perfectly with a sermon John read by Helmut Thielecke years ago. Thielecke, standing under the sky in the ruins of his church in Stuttgart, Germany, during World War II, and facing the aftermath of the horrific bombing of one of the most beautiful cities in Europe, spoke to the surviving half of his congregation. He knew they had questions, but if they asked the wrong question, they would get the wrong answer.

"Thielecke said 'why?' is the wrong question to ask God," John summarized. "It is a self-centered question. The right question is 'To what end? What purpose do you have for my life, God?'"

John immediately thought of those words when he learned he could have only four months to live, perhaps twenty with treatment. "I have never asked God why I have cancer. Instead I ask, 'to what end?'

"I'm learning to trust God for the day," John said. "We can be witnesses in a lot of ways. It can be through a miracle, suffering, and even death. I have come to realize that we walk in what we have. Whatever my time, like the roll call of faith in Hebrews, I only want to finish well. . . . Right now I am fearless in the hands of the Lord. It is a gift, and I want to walk in it for all the days the Lord gives to me."

John Eaves walked in faith every step of the way.

Sam House is editor-in-chief of HomeLife.

Your Life's Impact

John and Kay Eaves invested in the lives of people from different cultures as a way to show God's love in practical ways. Each of our lives has the potential to impact others with the love of God. And we can start with things we already like to do. For example:

- If you like to cook, host a monthly dinner party for your neighbors or serve in a local homeless shelter.
- If you like to use your hands, work with organizations like Habitat for Humanity.
- If you like to spend time with kids, babysit for a single mom at work or tutor through a local community center.
- If you like to shop, offer to go shopping for a shut-in.

The ways your life can impact others are as boundless as the love of God.

Chapter 2
The Emails Heard Around the World

Beginning in April 2003, John Eaves began to post periodic emails to friends, updating them on his condition, experiences, and perspective on his battle with cancer. To his surprise, people began to forward those emails around the world. John received emails and phone calls from people who were intrigued by the way in which he was facing cancer and the possibility of death. Throughout this process, John remained puzzled that anyone would find his response to cancer noteworthy. Nonetheless, he gave generously of his time and energy to respond to those who contacted him. As the rapidly spreading cancer took an increased toll on him, John was forced to stop responding to the emails and calls. Fortunately, his written record of emails now gives a permanent roadmap of the journey of faith he traveled. John always asked that we pray not for his recovery but that he might finish well.

Email 1: April 26, 2003
"Divine Inoculation for the Coming Storm"

Life is an incredible adventure of faith, as evidenced by the series of events that unfolded starting five days ago. For the past couple of months I have been having abdominal pain, and tests indicated that I had a polyp in my colon. When I had it removed, a tumor was discovered in another part of the colon. Evidently, it has been around a while, and the biopsy confirmed cancer. I will be having surgery in Nashville May 12th at Baptist Hospital, and I will stay in Nashville for at least six to eight weeks following surgery.

The encouragement I want to bring to you is starting about three weeks ago, the Lord started speaking strong words of exhortation to Kay and to me. In fact, one day I compared her email to my prayer journal entry back in March, and it was like a direct quote. In His marvelous grace, God was preparing us to stand firm in faith, almost like an inoculation, and to allow Him to fight the battle as we stand in a position of persevering faith. My biggest prayer at the moment is positioning ourselves in such a way that we discern how God is working in this specific context so we can direct our intercession accordingly.

In recent days, I have been looking at Paul's life as he advanced toward his destiny. When you read his final letters, like 2 Timothy and Philippians, Paul never gave up on life. He concerned himself with the practical details of his ministry to the very end. In fact, if anything, he accelerated toward his destiny, fully convinced of God's presence and deliverance. I want to be like that. I am writing you from New York City, trying to get things squared away. But I will return to Nashville on Thursday. You have shared in our lives for a long while, and our comfort is knowing the Lord has knit our lives together for such a time as this. Blessings on you.

Your Brother,
John Eaves

Email 2: May 6, 2003
"Facing Bad News—A Call to Prayer"

The quote of the day comes from Matthew, our son, when he said, "Dad, why don't you just quit going to the doctor. Every time you go they just give you bad news." We all chuckled at that profound insight. The CT scan yesterday revealed that the cancer in my body is far more advanced than was first thought. It has spread into the lymph nodes and liver. The interesting thing about this news is that as Kay and I were praying on Saturday, I found myself saying, "Lord, you can use us as your witnesses in all kinds of circumstances. We are your witnesses when you heal. We are your witness in suffering. We are witnesses even in death."

Many of you know that the last part of Hebrews 11 is one of my favorite passages. This role call of faith reminds us that God's leading in our lives may make us look to the world like an utter failure. But to Him, they are a beautiful testimony to faith that looks beyond circumstance. Right now, because of your prayers, I am fearless in the hands of the Lord. It is a gift, and I want to walk in it for all the days the Lord gives to me.

From a medical point of view, we are being asked to seek an oncological consult in order to assess what kind of chemotherapy approach would help slow down the advance of the cancer. We will weigh this out prayerfully. We will also need God's direction in terms of the best way to use our time. You know I have many dreams for ministry and new strategies that are to be rolled out in NYC. Some are already in process and entrusted to capable hands. Others are still a dream, but close to becoming a reality. I am anxious to see these dreams come true. Since I know you will want to focus your prayers, let me give you a few suggestions:

1) Pray for Kay. This is difficult news but God is at work in a wonderful way, and we are walking this road together as He has intended us to do.

2) Pray for Jesse, Joshua, and Matthew. Hard things in life provide an opportunity to build into us things that are not already there. That is exactly what God will do with these men of mine. I am confident of this.

3) Seek the Lord's guidance in how to pray for my body. You know, God loves these kind of odds, so don't look at the

outward circumstance as an indicator of how He is working. Believe me, He is working and it is wonderful. I know that many of you will want to help, and we will most definitely call on you when that time comes. I feel comfortable in doing that with you, because that is the kind of friendship we have. May Psalm 112:4–8 speak to your heart as it has to mine.

Blessings on you.

Your brother,
John Eaves

Email 3: May 13, 2003
"God's Preparation for these Days"

Yesterday we had a wonderful meeting with the oncologist, who was very helpful in defining where we are positioned in my unfolding health situation. Without going into too many details, the good news is it looks like surgery is now out of the picture. It seems that I am pretty far down the road in terms of the cancer's advancement in my body, so the game plan is to do chemo starting May 28, try to shrink the tumor, slow down the cancer in the rest of the body, and see if four months can be stretched into twenty. That is the medical side.

The spiritual side is much more exciting and engaging at the moment. Isn't it just like God to take what looks like a disaster and turn it into a blessing? That is exactly what is happening. Hearts are moved, lives touched, and God is on the move. I am praying that the days God gives will be some of the most meaningful in my life. I am not running to the sidelines. I am headed toward the center of the field.

Plans are still developing, but we can tell you some of the details:

1. The focus of this season of work for us will be centered in Nashville. I will have all of my medical work done here and will head for New York City with Kay to pick up my things sometime this week.

2. I know many of you thought that we were nuts in trying to operate in two sites—here in Nashville and NYC—for the past eighteen months. But what seemed to be crazy at first glance is now God's infinite love and grace at work. Kay has totally proven herself capable of running the entire ministry on her own because that is what she had to do with me setting things up in NYC. One of our colleagues recently shared that Kay has one of the most effective ministries around, and I would agree with that assessment. Last week, I felt like I was in a cafeteria buffet as international women moved in and out of our house all day long for Bible studies and small groups. What a gift this is from

the Lord, to know that He has prepared her in a way I never could have done.

3. Remember the story of the paralytic in Mark 2, who was lowered down in front of Jesus through the roof? Who did Jesus commend for such a tangible expression of faith? The paralytic? No, it was his friends. It seems that God is raising up stretcher-bearers that are bringing me before Jesus. These intercessors are not looking at circumstance, but fixing their eyes on the Lord alone. What a wonderful expression of the Body of Christ at work. I am learning how to let others carry the load.

Thank you for your prayers, emails, and cards, all of which remind us that the Lord has indeed blessed us beyond measure with friends like you.

All Our Love,
John Eaves

Email 4: May 26, 2003
"How God Transforms Tragedy into Ministry"

Do you remember the time I was given the opportunity to minister to rescue workers at Ground Zero after the World Trade Center attack? We decided to work in pairs, and my good friend Tim Pettit and I headed for the relief station in an elementary school adjacent to the smoldering hulk of Building #7. After talking with firefighters and phone workers for a few minutes, we came back outside. As I looked toward the wrecked building, I sensed in my spirit the Lord saying, "Go in there to the workers in the recovery area." I turned to Tim and said, "I think we are supposed to go in there."

Just as we started walking in that direction, there was a loud noise. In an instant, workers came streaming out of the building, running for their lives. If you have ever seen someone run for his life, you never forget the look on their face. They were terrified, and with good reason, because of possible collapse. So there we were, two guys with cleric collars watching this sea of humanity run past us. I guess we could have run with them, but we decided to wait a minute. When nothing happened, we moved forward. That decision opened two days of ministry on the other side of Building #7 to the people who needed it and welcomed it—the firefighters, police, and other workers at the site. Had we turned away, we would have missed it all.

I guess I feel the same way as I walk through the chemotherapy door this week. In my heart, I don't think this is so much about my treatments as about the people God wants us to meet. I noticed that I was assigned to "chair #8," so I ask you to pray for us to be His vessels of grace to the others who are sharing the same space and circumstance as I am, but maybe needing the kind of encouragement and hope that only the Lord can give in these situations. It may work the other way as well, as they encourage me.

I cannot begin to describe what a powerful and profound effect your prayers have been having. Thank you for loving us in this way.

Your brother in Christ,
John Eaves

Email 5: June 4, 2003
"Touching Lives in our Weakest Moments
in the Wilderness"

Over the years, I used to quote a statement from Oswald Chambers that a life crisis does not build anything new into our life at that moment of testing but simply reveals what is already there. My experience in recent weeks would perhaps modify that thought a bit. I would add that in our hour of testing, the follower of Jesus is given an ace up his or her sleeve—the Holy Spirit. In our moments of greatest weakness and vulnerability, the Lord comes to empower, comfort, and instill hope. Friday afternoon last week, I was struggling for the strength to sit in a chair after three days of chemo treatment. It was at that low point that I received one of the most beautiful gifts in my life.

My son Joshua had been sitting with me. Suddenly, he asked, "Dad, would you teach me the Bible?" The next day, Josh asked if three other friends could join us, so night before last we began a series on the Gospel of Mark. Ironically, one of the things we discussed on Tuesday from Mark 1 was the significance of the wilderness in the Scriptures. Throughout biblical history, the wilderness plays a huge role in God's interaction with His people. From Moses to Jesus, God calls His people into the wilderness. For us, it is a place of vulnerability, danger, and uncertainty. We are placed in an unfamiliar and hostile environment, where we see most clearly our inadequacy. But God never calls us into the wilderness without His provision. He meets with us in that desperate hour, reminding us of His precious promises and meeting our need. The wilderness becomes that place where danger and provision intersect with such incredible result. I think this captures my circumstance perfectly. In fact, we all encounter the wilderness experience several times during our lives. It is comforting to know that as followers of Jesus, we never go there alone.

I feel much stronger in terms of stamina this week, working through the entire day without having to stop and rest. I was able to meet several people from my chair

#8 position in the treatment room last week. Three of these were men in stage 4 like me, with colon cancer that was not detected until it had spread throughout the body. They were thirty-four and thirty-seven years old. We had a good conversation. I have learned how to disconnect the infusion machine from the wall and roll it around the room as it runs on batteries. Next Wednesday, when I go in for the second treatment, I hope to circulate a bit more throughout the treatment area. It is not an easy place to be, even with the Lord by your side. I can't imagine those who face such a circumstance without Him.

Do you remember me sharing about what a profound impact Hebrews 11:32–12:3 had on me in terms of gaining a perspective of being a witness for God in the context of miracles, hardships, and death? Last week, I was really pushing for an answer from the Lord as to which path I was to walk. On one of those mornings,

I got my answer, "I'm not going to tell you.
The discernment you are seeking I cannot
give, because I want you to trust me each
day . . . each moment." Isn't that just like
the Lord? No insider information . . . just
the eternal truth that each of us is called to
trust Him every day for our lives and well-
being.

God's peace be with you.

Thank you for continuing to stand with me,
John Eaves

Email 6: June 26, 2003
   "Dying Well for the Follower of Jesus"

You would think that a life measured
in months would take on a certain frantic
urgency. But when you place your life
in God's hands, you become more
comfortable with His pace in these matters.
Here, life deepens with an appreciation

for small things that we often overlook: pausing to thank, to encourage others, and being empowered to walk into hard places with a confidence you know is of a heavenly origin. Any way I look at it, I am a blessed man. Your cards, prayers, and encouraging words are all part of me being able to stand in this hour rather than to flee from it.

It seems that, for the most part, Christians in America struggle with how a man or woman in the Lord is to "die well." We don't get a lot of coaching on this topic, and that is unfortunate because knowing how to die as a believer helps us to live life to a fuller capacity. One of the first things I did after moving back from New York City was to help Kay and the family by taking care of the business of death. You may think this is rather morbid and indicates a lack of faith on my part for God to heal me. Nothing could be further from the truth. The truth is that when we prepare for death, we are then truly free to live. By me taking the initiative to revise wills, change car titles, and take care of funeral arrangements, I am expressing a tangible love for my family in doing what they should not have to do. Now that this aspect is cared for, I am free to explore all of the ministry opportunities God is bringing my way on a daily basis, to testify to the incredible dimensions of God's grace in the face of terminal illness. The reality of my condition is that for a follower of Jesus Christ, cancer never wins. It is never a question as to whether we will walk away from it or not, because we always will overcome it. The only remaining issue will be *in what body* – our earthly one or heavenly one. Either way, we win in Jesus, because He slam-dunked death.

I continue to be amazed at the opportunities God is bringing in this season. Some of you listen to Michael

Card's weekly radio show on the Moody Broadcasting Network called "In the Studio." It is a great program, and on Father's Day (the 6/14/03 show), I was interviewed by Mike. It was about forty-five minutes, and my interview was the second half of the show.

On another note, we know that chemo treatments tend to do a number on your hair, so you won't believe what it did for mine when you click on the attached picture. This was at Joshua's graduation last month. Do you think I could pass for a Bob Marley look-alike? I want to thank my "stretcher bearers" for continuing to lift me up before the Lord. Your prayers are doing a mighty work, and I praise God that His Body is doing what we were intended to do in bearing one another's burdens. You are awesome warriors.

All My Love,
John Eaves

Email 7: July 24, 2003
"Facing our Fears Daily and Vanquishing the Effects"

I just returned from the oncologist. The CT scan revealed that there has been a 50 percent reduction in the size of the tumors in both my liver and in my colon after the four chemo treatments I've undergone. The rate the cancer is spreading seems to have decreased about 45 percent since I started the treatments. I am feeling stronger too, even though the chemo treatments take their toll on energy levels. Let there be no doubt in your mind. Your prayers are making an incredible difference—not only for me, but also for all of the ministry opportunities that come my way each day as a result of my illness.

What does all of this mean? It seems to me that the Lord is lengthening my days and giving me a renewed strength so I can accomplish all He intends for my life. A couple of weeks ago my pastor came to the house and prayed a prayer I feel best captures my heart. He asked that God would enable me to accomplish all the good works He intends me to walk in and for none of them to be shortened. I say "amen" to that prayer.

Lately, I have been reflecting on the whole issue of fear. Fear has an incredible capacity to eat away at faith. I think it is amazing how one minute we can be going along with a reasonable sense of self-confidence, then the next moment we are slammed by a circumstance that practically paralyzes us in our tracks. Why is it that when fear strikes, faith goes out the window? Rebecca Pippert, in her recent book entitled *A Heart for God,* states:

The silver lining in the dark cloud of fear is that fear pushes us to decide on our view of reality. What do I truly believe

*about the universe? Am I alone in this
battle, or is there a God who overrules
human affairs? Does my deliverance
depend upon human prowess and things I
can see, or does the final outcome depend
on a massive resource beyond my own—
the powerful, faithful, living God?*[1]

What I have discovered is that I do
not need more *self*-confidence but *God*-
confidence. Many of you have commented
about my strong stand of faith in the midst
of facing a terminal illness. My confidence
is not my own. It stems from trusting
that God is who He says He is, and that
when He says He will be a present help
in all our troubles, He means it and acts
accordingly. It's just like the comment a
friend shared with me last weekend when
he said that the 23rd Psalm is not a hope
of David, nor even a prayer. Rather, it is a
statement of fact about God's character
and nature. The Lord is our shepherd. He

leads us through the valley of the shadow of death. We never have to fear evil. He will restore our soul and guide us in paths of righteousness. This is who God is. One thing I know is that where God leads, that is where we find life. It is found nowhere else.

Thank you for continuing to hold me up before the Lord with your prayers and expressions of love and concern. You have loved well.

In Jesus's Love,
John Eaves

Email 8: August 11, 2003
"Resting Faith"

I could not have been more blessed than by this past weekend. On Friday Ji Li, from China, and Lisa Chen, from Taiwan, flew to Nashville for me to marry them Friday night. I can't begin to tell you how much joy this brought to our hearts, because of our love for this wonderful couple and a friendship that dates back to 1992 when Ji was a student at Vanderbilt. It was so much fun planning the wedding too, from flowers to reception.

I then preached three times on Saturday evening and twice on Sunday morning on the topic "Finishing Well: How a Follower of Jesus Faces Living and Dying." Then last night, we had a "thanksgiving" dinner with thirty of our African friends who had banded together to pray for one of our dear friend's child from Rwanda who had cancer, and for me. We sang, prayed, and ate dinner in honor of God's working in our lives. What a blessed weekend for us.

Today, I had my sixth chemo treatment. It was great meeting a woman who has been battling colon cancer for seven years. When I told her the work I do, she responded by saying, "I want to talk with you about the religious aspect to what I am going through. I feel like my life has not accounted for much." I unplugged my IV pole, let it run on batteries, and sat down for a nice chat.

Friday afternoon I had an incredible experience. I was taking a short nap in preparation for the wedding that evening, and as I was lying in bed, two words came to mind—"resting faith." In the Scriptures, we really do see two kinds of faith. The first is what I would call "active faith." It is the kind of faith that is exhibited by fasting, perseverance, and tenacity for seeking God with all of your heart, mind, strength, and soul. It is a faith that blasts right past circumstance and grabs hold of the horns of the altar, as it were. But the Lord reminded me of a second kind of faith—a resting faith. It is the kind of faith we see exhibited by Paul in prison in Philippians 4:11–13 about learning to be content in all circumstances. It is the faith exhibited in Daniel 3:17–18 when Shadrach, Meshach, and Abednego said to the king, who was about to execute them in the flames, saying, "We know that God will deliver us, but even if He doesn't we will still not worship the image you have set up to worship." It is a faith that knows, that knows, that knows, and rests in the hands of our Lord. This is what God has so graciously given to me. I can rest in Him because I know the stretcher bearers He has given me are seeking His face on my behalf. There are days when I get up and I feel like there are arms holding me up, and I know that is you all through your intercession. Thank you so much for your tenacity and perseverance in prayer. I am indeed a blessed man.

All our Love,
John Eaves

Email 9: August 29, 2003
"God's Deliverance—
From our Trials and Through our Trials"

How thankful I am for this season of increased strength. Preaching five times in the last three weeks, conducting a wedding for wonderful friends from China and Taiwan, and setting up for our fall ministry programming should give you some idea of how your prayers are being answered. It is incredible how the Lord has used this illness to allow me to come alongside others who are walking the same path. It was something I did not anticipate, but I am making the most out of the opportunities for bringing testimony to the fact that God's grace is sufficient for any and every life trial. I have come to see that God can deliver us in two ways—He delivers us *from* our trials and He delivers us *through* our trials. It is an important distinction, because I think we tend to opt for the first option, so when the second one comes our way we are somehow caught off guard and start questioning where God is in our hour of need. This is perhaps why we tend to focus on ourselves when we encounter life trials. I am not doing that, and it is solely because of His grace working through me. Recently, I was reading Michael Card's new book on the apostle Peter, entitled *A Fragile Stone*. Michael was reflecting on Peter's sinking in the water. He says:

Why did Peter doubt? After all, he had begun to accomplish it, he had walked on the water. But there was a deeper lesson he had to learn, and Jesus was intent on him not missing it, even as now you and I must learn it if we are to move forward as we walk through the wind storm of following Jesus . . . The lesson is that Peter needed to sink in order to take the next step of faith in Jesus. Because walking on water does not ultimately increase our faith, only sinking does! Those who ask for miracles and receive them soon forget. But those who suffer for Christ's sake never forget. They have their own wounds to remind them. When we are hurting, we do not flee to the rich and healthy for wisdom and real comfort. We seek out those who have fellowshipped in the sufferings of Jesus.[2]

Mike's insights are so true in this situation as emails and phone calls come daily from those who are walking through the valley of the shadow of death, or who have loved ones in that situation. I am praying that the Lord will continue to open these opportunities for ministry and for me to keep a humbled heart that cries out for more of Him and less of me. As I write this, I am on my seventh chemo treatment. The current plan is to do one more treatment and take another CT scan to see what's happening with the primary tumor in the colon and the multiple tumors in the liver and lymph nodes. There is a possibility for surgery to remove the primary tumor, but it is somewhat remote. My approach is to take each day and run with it as far as I can. We are incredibly blessed to walk this road together with you. You are the burden bearers that Paul praises in Galatians 6:2, and for this I am truly a blessed man.

Your brother in Christ,
John Eaves

Email 10: September 25, 2003
"How Illness Moves Us to the Center Rather than the Sidelines"

I just walked in the door from the oncologist's [office]. The good news for me is I get a month break from chemotherapy. Testing revealed that two tumors had continued to reduce, while one had slightly increased in size. The level of cancer activity has also increased a bit from previous results, leading to the conclusion that the drug combination I was on had probably reached its level of effectiveness. I felt it was a good time to give the body a breather.

I am in great spirits, and am so excited to celebrate my 50th birthday this weekend. I am celebrating in a big way by having a party with friends, because back in April I was not at all certain that I would make it to my birthday. But here I am, rejoicing in the life God gives. One discovers in such times just how important hope is in our lives. Hope is a paradox, because it is future-based and past-based at the same time. We know we can trust the Lord for our future because of His faithfulness in the past. I think that is why I so appreciate Paul's attitude in his life trial while imprisoned in Rome in Philippians 1:19–26. Eugene Peterson captures his thoughts best by paraphrasing Paul in this way:

On the contrary, everything happening to me in this jail only serves to make Christ more accurately known, regardless of whether I live or die. They didn't shut me up; they gave me a pulpit! Alive, I'm Christ's messenger; dead, I'm his bounty. Life versus even more life! I can't lose. (MSG)

That's the way I feel today. I can't lose when I am with Jesus. Cancer in my body is only serving to make Jesus known to those who are searching for an authentic experience with God. I never in a thousand years would have imagined such incredible opportunities to come alongside others who are walking this same path, but the truth is that empowerment in ministry comes through personally identifying with those we are seeking to love. Perhaps that is why Jesus was always so attractive to me, because He was willing to so thoroughly identify with those He sought to love. He did it then. He does it now. Thank you so much for your prayers, which are accomplishing more than we could ever ask or imagine.

Your brother in Christ,
John Eaves

Email 11: October 9, 2003
"Issues of Healing: The Nature of Faith in God's Economy"

Kay and I have just returned from a long weekend in New York City, reconnecting with friends and keeping a check on the pulse of the ministry that continues in our absence. It was in my heart to have God use me in NYC to raise up the next generation of leaders

for serving Him, but I did not realize
that the transition schedule was to be so
accelerated. Our staff is doing a wonderful
job, and I am so proud of their efforts.
My heart for New York City remains, and I
hope someday to be given the opportunity
to return.

You know, I don't think a lot about
cancer. In a very untypical manner, I have
had little interest in doing a lot of research,
or seeking after a variety of therapy
options. Frankly, I have other things I would
rather be doing in terms of carrying on a
ministry. Why? Because God can heal me
without my help. This illness is not about
me. It is about Him.

Recently a woman called me who
had heard about my sermon on being a
witness for Jesus in our trials and in the
way we die. She has been diagnosed with
terminal cancer. I remember one particular
statement she made to me. She said that
she had tried just about every alternative

cancer therapy possible and four different diets. "The problem I have," she said, "is that it all seems to be about me and what I do to make myself better." She said that she had told God that she had recently given the whole thing over to Him out of sheer frustration. I told her that her decision was really the starting point rather than the ending point. God never intends for us to walk this road of life alone. Faith does not have to deny the facts. I am sick. I have a terminal disease. God does not want me to deny it or pretend like it does not exist. Rather, He wants me to trust Him and leave the matter in His hands.

Last week I was given the opportunity to share about going through life's trials with seventy students in high school. I reminded them, as I reminded the woman caller, that God never intended for us to go through life alone, and brought them back to a familiar psalm they had probably memorized as a child. It begins with "the Lord is my shepherd." Park on that phrase for a while, and you begin to understand that illness is God's battle, not ours. Deliverance can take us from the trial, but it can also lead us through it. David does not say "*if* I walk through the shadow of death, I will fear no evil." He says "*when* I walk . . ." As our shepherd, God releases us from fear because He is the one watching the front and back doors of our lives. Being released from fear is perhaps the greatest gift of all, and it has already been done for those who trust in Jesus. Listen to the writer of Hebrews 2:14–15 speak about our Shepherd:

Since the children have flesh and blood, he too shared in their humanity so that by his death he might destroy him who holds the power of death—that is, the devil—and free those who all their lives were held in slavery by their fear of death.

My prayer is that God will indeed free you from all fear, even the fear of death. For when we are not afraid to die, we become free to live.

Your brother in Christ,
John Eaves

Email 12: October 24, 2003
"Living Life Through the Eyes of Eternity"

Sometimes I wonder in what ways knowing that I have a terminal disease affects the way I relate to the medical community. I remember my first chemo treatment, listening to my fellow cancer club members talk to their nurse, inquiring about red blood cell counts, CEA readings, and the like. At the time it seemed a bit extreme. But now I understand why they were doing that—because life for the terminal cancer patient has a way of centering around how we are feeling, and the diagnostic tests and blood draws are used to confirm what we usually already know in terms of gaining ground or losing it. The question is how one is supposed to handle bad news when you seem to be getting the short end of the stick.

Yesterday, the oncologist confirmed that my time off of chemotherapy came at a price. The liver tumors have doubled in size in four weeks; blood counts are down; cancer activity is up. I think we can classify that as bad news. What does news like this do to those of you who are praying so fervently for God's healing of my body? What does it do to me? I can answer for both of us. It should do nothing. Our life circumstance is but one component to being a follower of Jesus. God has other life components that take higher priority. Listen to how the apostle Paul describes this truth:

So we're not giving up. How could we! Even though on the outside it often looks like things are falling apart around us, on the inside, where God is making new life, not a day goes by without His unfolding grace. . . . The Spirit of God whets our appetite by giving us a taste of what's ahead. He puts a little of heaven in our hearts so that we'll never settle for less.

That's why we live with such good cheer. You won't see us drooping our heads or dragging our feet! . . . It's what we trust in but don't yet see that keeps us going. Do you suppose a few ruts in the road or rocks in the path are going to stop us? When the time comes, we'll be plenty ready to exchange exile for homecoming.

But neither exile nor homecoming is the main thing. Cheerfully pleasing God is the main thing, and that's what we aim to do, regardless of the conditions. (2 Cor. 4:16, 5:5–10 MSG)

Paul understands what it means to live life through the eyes of eternity, rather than thinking all there is to our existence is what happens in this body of ours. Faith gives us the capacity to view human reality from God's point of view rather than our own. It is what gives us the ability to rightly measure life circumstance as only a small piece of a much bigger picture. This is what gives us the hope to walk through our trials rather than cave into them in bitterness and disappointment.

Any normal person wants to hear good news rather than bad. You and I would probably be much happier today if I told you that there is no evidence of cancer in my body. But how far would that miracle take us? Mind you, I am still ready for God to heal my body. I have no doubt in His capacity to do so. Yet as a follower of Jesus, I see my life in a fuller light. The paradox of walking with Jesus is that faith grows better in trial than in ease. I don't look for troubles in life, but when they come, I stand in a God-given confidence and peace that is perhaps just as great a witness to a watching world as to be delivered from it all. Faith builds upon faith, and I am a blessed man today to stare bad news in the face and not be discouraged. It is a gift indeed.

Your brother in Christ,
John Eaves

Email 13: November 13, 2003
"Standing in the Pain"

Lately I have been experiencing increased pain in my liver and a fatigue that feels like the worst case of flu you ever had. The cancer advances. Do you know what pain does to you? It tries to neutralize two areas in the life of a follower of Jesus.

Pain takes aim at faith and courage, the two things we need so much and count on. Faith and courage are like manna. God provides them when you need them in the moment. The problem is that pain makes you do all sorts of weird things because it provides a breeding ground for fear, and fear can set you off in directions you never would have considered. It tempts you to grasp at anything you can get a hold of, like a drowning swimmer who latches onto his or her rescuer in the panic of the moment. Is there anything God has given us that can provide an anchor point when faith and courage are compromised? Yes, I believe there is. It is hope.

Over the thirty years I have followed Jesus, He has always shown Himself to be a faithful Savior. I do not use the word "always" lightly. I mean what I say. God has always been there for me and for my family, and He has come through with what He knew I needed. The result is that I simply have too much history with the Lord to doubt Him. You might not feel that way. Maybe you have not followed Him for a long period of time, or maybe things did not go the way you wanted, so you questioned His love and His presence in your life. But if you do what pastor and writer Eugene Peterson suggests in his book entitled *A Long Obedience In the Same Direction*, then you begin to discover the remarkable mercy and love and faithfulness of Jesus's presence. What is this obedience? It is simple trust in a Savior who has lavished on us an indescribable love and grace that transforms us from the inside out.

Different people have different thresholds of pain. Mine happens to be low. I am not quite sure if that is a gift or a burden. I guess it depends on the circumstance. A low pain threshold signals earlier on that something is wrong with your body. But it also makes you miserable for a longer period of time. I guess it is somewhat of a tradeoff. But one thing I do know: pain is real. We are not called to deny that it exists. You will not hear me report that things are going great when I am biting my lip. At the same time, I will not hesitate to counter-attack with prayer. I am not ashamed to take medication to help me to better tolerate the pain. But above all, I have a wonderful safety net, and I will fall into it over and over again. I will fall into the hands of Jesus, my hope. Some days, that is all you can do.

A close family friend from Uganda came over today to visit. As we were talking, she told me how hens in Uganda will gather the chicks under their wings when the hawk flies overhead, and they will keep them there until danger passes. She quoted Psalm 91:4.

He will cover you with his feathers, and under his wings you will find refuge; his faithfulness will be your shield and rampart.

May we run under his wings and stay there, even after danger passes.

Your brother in Christ,
John Eaves

Email 14: December 2, 2003
"The Final Word: Finishing the Race Well"

Who gets to speak the final word about matters of life and of death? The one who gives us life in the first place—Jesus. If you believe, as I do, that life is not about us but about Jesus and our faithful witness for Him, then you come to understand why Hebrews 11:32–12:3 gives us the most accurate and realistic view of the Christian walk in all of the Bible. It has been the track that God has given me to run on these past seven months, and has yet to fail me in matters of encouragement and discerning God's hand at work through difficult circumstances that potentially fog our view. We are indeed His witnesses . . . in the miracles He brings, through our trials and hardships, even in the way we die.

Looking back to last April, I have greatly benefited from the wonderful role many of you have faithfully performed as my "stretcher-bearers" (see Mark 2:1–12) in bringing your requests for my healing before the throne of God. You did not passively sit on the sidelines, but fully engaged in the business of bearing up a dying man so he could focus on other ministry opportunities. Yet I am a bit concerned for you today. I wonder how you will bear up when you learn that God did not answer your prayers for my healing

in the way you thought He would. I don't
want you to become discouraged. Prayer
always has, and will be, a powerful and
effective weapon in the hands of Jesus's
followers. You and I will never fully know
all that God accomplished by taking your
healing prayers and translating them into
a spiritual force that has sustained me
physically, emotionally, and spiritually these
last several months.

Prayer for the sick and dying is
not about getting it right. It is about
persevering with God. While we never get
God's will "spot on" all the time, we never
stop pressing into that will. Who of us has
ever shown a measure of success in trying
to force God's hand to perform the way
we want Him to? When I try, I discover
the faith produced in me is counterfeit: an
immature and weakened version of what
He really wants. What this chapter of life
has taught me is that heaven and earth

move in prayer. That is enough motivation for me to pick up the stretcher over and over and over again.

Last night, I spoke to an African fellowship. These are dear friends from Rwanda and neighboring east-African nations, with whom we have been blessed to walk together in a community of faith these past twelve years. When I rose to speak, I was so physically weak that I wanted to cry. I decided against it because it would take more energy than just feeling bad. The text I shared was Paul's thorn in the flesh. My point was that God can have us pray for a particular thing, but can answer it in a manner entirely different from the request. It only took Paul three times to figure that out. God reminded him from his own ministry that the power of God is best displayed in wounded warriors, not healthy ones. It is the wounded ones who know best their need of God. The healthy ones all too frequently strike out on their own and ask God to bless their efforts on His behalf. Ironic, but true: the paradox of weakness.

The real lesson of the evening came during the sharing time. One woman from Rwanda said, "When we went through the genocide in 1994, all we tried to do was to survive. We had no spiritual perspective on what was happening. But now, God has chosen John to be a living example of how we are to walk in faith through life's trials. All these months, you have been teaching us through your life these truths. Because you walked through these hardships, we now have a way of understanding God's presence and work in our own lives' struggles."

Terminal illness has a way of turning us in on ourselves. We just can't help it. But God had other plans for me. His call on my life was to come alongside you, as the Body of Christ, and the sick and the dying.

He used my incredible weakness of spirit
and body to pour out His power as a living
witness to Him and as a living example of
how He can help us to finish well.

Last week, I spoke for what will
probably be the last time in a church here
in Nashville. The first service, I was so
weak that I had to sit during part of the
sermon. But when I rose to speak in the
second service, a power and energy shot
through me like a bullet. It shocked me.
The first words that came out of my mouth
were delivered with power and conviction,
like another person doing the speaking for
me. Toward the end of the service, I was
talking about Hebrews 2:14–15 and how
Jesus has freed us from the fear of death
that had held us hostage all of our lives.
In a spontaneous moment of inspiration,
I told the congregation about the scene
in the movie *Braveheart* when William
Wallace, against all odds, won a battle
against the English army. Mel Gibson, who

was playing the Wallace character, thrust his sword into the air and gave one of the most gut-busting yells of triumph from the very bowels of his being I have ever heard. I asked the congregation to stand, and declared, "Today, we are claiming our victory over the fear of death." When I counted to three, much to my delight, Mel Gibson was upstaged by a bunch of Presbyterians! Our yell pierced the gates of hell and heaven.

I have openly shared my journey of faith with you these past seven months. Only God knows the full number of my days in this body, and I believe I have said all He has wanted me to share. Let me leave you with a Bible passage that has touched a core spiritual nerve in my life. I still can't read it without getting tears in my eyes and a lump in my throat, even after thirty years of practice. I guess I knew early on it was to be part of my spiritual destiny in the Lord. Paul says:

For I am already being poured out like a drink offering, and the time has come for my departure. I have fought the good fight, I have finished the race, I have kept the faith. Now there is in store for me the crown of righteousness, which the Lord, the righteous Judge, will award to me on that day—and not only to me, but also to <u>all</u> who have longed for his appearing. (2 Tim. 4:6–8, emphasis added)

I am indeed a happy and blessed man. Life simply does not get any better than this, at least not on this side of heaven. Grace and peace to you.

Your brother in Christ,
John Eaves

Email 15: January 22, 2004
"God's Game Plan in Silence"

Yesterday could have been a day of crushing. It arrived, right on schedule. But I don't think it had the intended effect. After a series of extended tests, the oncologist said all medical interventions to date had failed. The tumors continue to grow unchecked. There were experimental options, but unlike other oncologists who simply can't say enough is enough, my doctor agrees with my philosophy of not suffering twice for the same disease (the cancer and the chemo with its side effects). He simply said, "I am taking you off of chemo treatments." How would you personally receive those words? My prayers had focused on getting a definitive answer one way or the other. The glass had stayed half-empty and half-full for over four months, and I really wanted to know where things were headed. This expression of impatience is common for those members of the chemo club and cancer club. We want to know where we stand in the battle.

From a human viewpoint, it looked like a major defeat. One big slam-dunk for Satan. Something akin to Jesus hanging on the cross. Things came to a complete stop on the hill. Satan gloated over how easy it was to take out the Son of God. He lost focus, not aware of things happening in other locations around the city and in heaven. Because about the same time I was getting my news, a high school senior was weighing out his life after reading John Eldredge's *Wild at Heart*. His conclusion was to wholly commit his life to Jesus and to serve him like his parents had done. That person was my son Matthew.

What did my disease bring? The raising up of a new generation wholly committed to Jesus as their Lord. It was the gift a father can wait a lifetime to see, and when it comes, there is no greater blessing than to walk in that moment. Thank God for the countless victories He has won through my cancer and God calling me to walk through it as His witness. God has been silent for the last several weeks, while the pain increased and my ability to walk steadfastly in the Lord was more and more difficult. I am not afraid of the silence of God. The flip side of silence is frequently an expression of trust in us. It sounds weird, but what is there about the Christian life that is "normal" by the world's standards? Trust expressed by one person frequently elicits trust from the second person involved. That is why I open myself to risking for the Lord in following His guidance and directives in my life. This is what my generation needs more of. We are not sent here to protect assets but to risk them for Jesus. I am not at all set back. Rather I need you to live out this truth: It's not over until it is over.

• I want to see Matthew graduate the last of May. Pray me there.

• I want God to get His glory alone in bringing me to complete healing and restoration. Intercede as He gives you the faith to do so.

Don't feel guilty if you find it difficult to pray for what seems in human reality to be a lost cause. Move on with life, and allow God to build a passion and faith in Him. If you are still that tenacious "stretcher bearer," press into the Lord to better hear His voice on how He would have you specifically pray.

All our Love,
John Eaves

Email 16: Date Unknown
"What Does Heaven Look Like Now?"

A few days ago a friend ask me if I had been thinking more about heaven, and if so, what was I thinking? I realized that the Lord had changed the way I now answer such a question. The Bible only gives us brief snapshots of heaven and the transition from one location to the next. Bible commentators have done a pretty good job in detailing certain aspects regarding appearance and some kind of timetable. I now take a different approach to the question, because the answer must reflect our belief in seeing life today through the eyes of eternity. Do you want to really know what the transition from this earthly reality into a heavenly reality is all about? It is simply another day.

Don't be shocked. It's true. If we, as believers, are living our lives through the eyes of eternity, then our death and transition to be with the Lord in heaven is another day in this road we are walking through eternity. Oh sure, things look different—very different, in fact. Yet in that difference resides a sameness as well. I am still me in spirit. Jesus is still Jesus. Relations are, at least in heaven's timetable, temporarily changed with the saints continuing to do God's work on earth. Old relationships are now reunited. Never mind the timetable to all of this. With the Lord a day is like a thousand years, and a thousand years as a day (Psalm 90:4). The beauty of the resurrection life is that, as always, we remain firmly in God's loving hands. Another day of witnessing and living out His Divine faithfulness. There is no fear, for in the eyes of eternity, today is just another day.

Chapter 3

Finishing Well

A Sermon on Learning to Live Through Terminal Illness

by John Eaves

West End Community Church,
Nashville, Tennessee
November 23, 2003

L ife is not about us. Life is about
Jesus and our witness for Him in
this world. It has taken me a lifetime
to embrace this fundamental truth in all of
its implications. It has also taken the same
amount of time to recognize that our witness
for Jesus is frequently manifested in our
absolute weakest moments rather than when

we are at full strength. My weakest moment began this past April. I guess I did find it somewhat strange to wake up from what was to be a routine colonoscopy to remove a polyp and find my family doctor standing beside me. His office was in another building. Why would he want to meet me when I awoke from my procedure to remove a simple colon polyp? I was soon to learn there was more. My regular doctor said, "John, we found a tumor. It looks like cancer." The GI doctor standing next to him sounded a bit more optimistic. Speaking in a unique Tennessee-cowboy dialect, he said, "Not to worry son. We'll lasso that thang and yank it outta there lickity split. You're gonna be just fine." That phrase "you will be fine" was never spoken again after that day. Further tests revealed stage 4 metastatic cancer originating in the colon, simmering undetected for eight or nine years. Only recently had it apparently spread to other vital organs. There was never any mention of "cure" either. Rather, I was assigned to a category called "palliative care patient," which is a nice way of saying that we can try to keep you comfortable and extend your days through chemo treatments. But we will never be able to heal you.

In some ways, my diagnosis stands against all who thought that life was about being fair when it came to our health. So many of us, believer and non-believer alike, have bought into the unconscious assumption that if we eat right and live right and take good care of ourselves, we will be rewarded with long life. In some ways, it continues to amaze me how many people think this way. It sounds so plausible, but in reality it is a lie. Why? Because this belief is based on our belief that we have the capacity to control our destiny, and the truth is we have no such control.

All of us have come face to face with death or suffering at one time or another. If you are like most people, you get stumped on an incredibly simple question—*Why?* Such an innocent word, only three letters, yet filled with unresolved anger, bitterness, and confusion. We all want to ask it, and none of us gets the answer we are looking for. I am thankful that I never asked that question, because of a simple sermon I read more than twenty-five years ago by a German pastor named Helmut Thielecke. While pastoring a church in Stuttgart, Germany, in 1944, an allied bombing wiped out almost half of his congregation and heavily damaged the sanctuary in which the church members gathered each week. The next day, a remnant of the congregation met in the bombed out sanctuary. Pushing back the rubble to make a place to sit, the congregation listened to Pastor Thielecke deliver one of the most significant sermons in their entire lives. I am paraphrasing here, but I think you will get the message he was trying to convey:

I know the question many of you want to ask this morning. But I want to remind you that if you ask the wrong question, you will inevitably receive the wrong answer. Today "why" is the wrong question to ask. The reason is that at the core of this simple three letter word is an attitude of self-centeredness. The focus is on ourselves, not on God. Life did not go as we anticipated, and we insist on knowing why it did not. The better question to ask in such a situation is "to what end?" That is a question God can answer and can work with, because we are focusing on God rather than ourselves. This is a question He longs to answer for us this morning.

Some of you this morning are still stuck on the "why" question. You have become embittered, angry, and refuse God's repeated attempts to lead you through the valley of trial to a place of rest and provision. You have created your own hell of self-pity, and you insist on keeping yourself in this self-imposed state of mind. Come out! Come out, now! Simply ask the right question and see what God will do by shifting your focus from yourself to Him.

God is so amazing in preparing us for trials and hardships in life. In my case, weeks before I knew anything about cancer, my quiet times were filled with words of admonition and encouragement to stand firm, to allow the Lord to fight our battles, and to trust Him in all things. After my diagnosis, Kay and I were praying together one night. I was shocked by my prayer, because it was like someone else was praying it. I said, "Lord, I know there are a lot of ways we can be a witness for you. We can be a witness in your miracles you perform in our lives; we can be a witness in walking through trials and hardship; we can even be a witness in the way we die." The next morning, I returned to a favorite passage of mine—Hebrews 11:32–12:3. As you know, biblical scholars know this chapter as the roll call of faith. It is an attempt by the writer to look over our shoulders and remember all that God has done through his people over the centuries, and of His faithfulness to us as His people. What I find fascinating about this passage is that in many ways it is the most realistic view of the Christian life in the Bible. Why? Because it presents life as it really is for a follower of Jesus rather than how we would want it to be—full of ease, prosperity, and blessing.

The first few sentences in the paragraph are predictable. Miracles are performed—the dead raised to life, people delivered from certain death. It is an incredibly powerful encounter with God when he breaks into human circumstance. Suddenly, the tone changes beginning in the second part of Hebrews 11:35. God's people are being openly violated, persecuted, tortured, beaten, and killed for their faith. They are deprived of earthly comforts, disoriented, and destitute. Many die, for no other reason than identifying themselves as servants of God and following His directives. Could it be that we in America have been sold short when it comes to understanding the Christian life in the fullness it represents? Yes, we have. We seek the easy way. We forget that throughout biblical history, trials, hardship, and death are equally a part of our witness to an unbelieving world as healing and deliverance and Divine blessing. This passage unwraps three paths of witness for the follower of Jesus, which we will examine together this morning:

1. Our witness through God's miracles

2. Our witness through trials and hardship

3. Our witness in the way we die

As followers of Jesus, we embrace the miraculous. God loves to work with circumstances with labels like "impossible," "terminal," and "hopeless." In my case, I am very open-handed with God healing me, even this very moment. There is absolutely no question in my mind that He can do it, and I am ready to receive this form of grace. But I don't demand it. I don't insist on my way being His way of handling my current circumstance. That is one foolish line of thinking—in taking His promises He gave us and forcing His hand to do my bidding. In the same manner, contrary to a lot of TV teaching on the issue of faith and healing, I also do not think my healing is solely about my faith and me. I do not think Jesus will have a conversation with me in heaven saying, "John, I would have healed you, but your faith quotient was only 48 percent and you needed a 50 percent minimum to pass," or "I would have healed you if you just would have gone to the Benny Hinn or Kenneth Hagin healing conference."

As I read the Scriptures, I notice something striking about Jesus and healing. Roughly half the time Jesus makes some comment regarding the faith of the person he has healed. But the other times, he just healed people with no pre-condition whatsoever. Today, there is a lot of bad teaching floating around on healing. One particularly devastating teaching is to have a person prayed over, healing claimed, and then nothing more be said about the illness. I met such a woman a few months ago. Like me, she had terminal cancer. With tears in her eyes, she recounted how, as a mother of five children, she had undergone all kinds of alternate treatments in Mexico, four diets for cancer healing, and a multitude of other advice. "I simply cannot do this anymore," she said, "because I realize that everything I have tried is all about me. It is about how I am going to take control over my own healing. I just can't do that anymore. I told God I was at the end of my rope and gave it over to Him." Do you know what I told her? I said, "That is not the end. It is the beginning. All this time, the Lord has wanted you to place this disease in His hands, not your own." I also told her that because of the poor teaching she had received on healing, her family was going to be the ones to suffer the most. It will be her kids who say, "Mommy died because we didn't have enough faith for mommy to be healed."

"Is that the kind of baggage you want to leave on your family?" I asked.

"No," she said. I thought it was a breakthrough. But several weeks later I learned she was back in Mexico at a clinic for alternate cancer treatments. How simple a transaction it is to put our life in God's hands, yet how complicated we make it by keeping our hands on the controls.

The right attitude about miracles and God's breaking into our lives is simply to trust Him. This may sound too easy for you. Trust is the practical outworking of faith, and Jesus was the first to remind us of this important truth. Do you remember the conversation the disciples had with Jesus about who was the greatest in the kingdom of heaven? Jesus drew a child standing close to him in his arms, and said, "Unless you change and become like little children, you will never enter the kingdom of heaven" (Matt. 18:3). Jesus knew that without a complete reworking of our adult view of faith, we are hopelessly lost. And what is the essence of a child-like faith? Is it not unreserved trust?

Faith has two distinct expressions for the follower of Jesus. The first we can call an "active faith." This is the one we are most accustomed to, and to which most teaching on healing tends to camp out. It is a tenacious faith, holding on and holding out until God responds. The persistent widow is the poster child of this kind of faith, and Jesus Himself uses her in a parable to teach us to persevere in our prayers and to not give up (Luke 18:1–8).

However, the second biblical expression of faith is equally viable and necessary. It is a "resting faith"; a faith that knows . . . that it knows . . . that it knows. It is the faith we see expressed in Daniel 3:17–18 when Shadrach, Meshach, and Abednego said to the king of Babylon, "the God we serve is able to . . . rescue us from your hand, O king. But even if he does not, . . . we will not serve your gods." It is the faith credited as righteousness

to Abraham when he believed God for a son
in his old age (Gen. 15:6). This is the faith
God has imparted into my life. I am resting in
His daily provision, never insisting on things
going my way, but His. It is a yielded life, a
surrendered life, which intimately becomes a
transformed life (Rom. 8:28–30).

To those here this morning who are not
sick or suffering, how does God intend to
use you as a member of the Body of Christ to
minister to those in need? To the terminally
ill, words like, "If there is anything I can do . . ."
have absolutely zero effect. Nada. Zippo. An
offer to do anything is an offer to do nothing,
and we who are sick know it better than you
who are well. Fortunately, there is a biblical
alternative. Do you remember the story of
the paralytic in Mark 2:1–12? His friends had
brought him to Jesus to be healed, but the
crowd was simply too large to get him close.
Instead of giving up, they hoisted him up on
the roof, tore a big hole in it, and lowered
their friend in front of Jesus. Do you know

what Jesus did? He commended the faith of the paralytic's friends! These stretcher-bearers made sure their friend was kept in front of Jesus through their persevering efforts.

It reminds me of the time I was in Uganda in the most remote part of that country. On a mountain opposite us, I saw a line of people, perhaps twenty-five or thirty. In front of them was a stretcher, and every few minutes, the procession would stop, and the stretcher-bearers would rotate to the back of the line and a fresh set of bodies would take up the burden. They were taking their friend to the clinic twenty miles away, but they were only able to do so when the village came together to help.

God wants us to be stretcher-bearers for one another. I think this is exactly what Paul had in mind when he said, "Carry each other's burdens, and in this way you will fulfill the law of Christ" (Gal. 6:2). I don't have to worry about my healing, because God has given me wonderful stretcher-bearers in the Body of

Christ to carry my needs before Him every day. This is how the Body of Christ works. Anything less is counterfeit community. It is a costly service, but genuine through and through. As Arthur McGill states in his book *Suffering: A Test of Theological Method*:

A man only begins to love as Jesus commands when he gives out of what is essential to him, out of what he cannot "afford." For Jesus, it is the deliberate and uninhibited willingness to expend oneself for another that constitutes love.[3]

The second witness we have in this world is through trials and hardship. God delivers His people in two ways: He delivers us *from* our trials, and He delivers us *through* our trials. The interesting thing is we do not have a choice as to which path we travel. Have you ever noticed that when you get sick or face hardships of one kind or another the focal point of attention seems to rest on yourself? One of the great lessons I learned through my illness is that God will frequently call us to come alongside others who are facing the same circumstance we are. I call it "incarnational illness." God deliberately intersects our lives with the hurting at the very moment when we hurt. Why does He do this? Because He knows that weakness is the perfect soil for growing dependence in Him. Stripped of our own gifts and resources, we are perfectly positioned to trust Him.

You might be surprised to hear this, but I did not take chemotherapy because I thought it would help me. I had resolved in my heart to never suffer twice for the same disease. When chemo treatments became more painful than the cancer, that was to be my signal to stop. The day before my first treatment I spent time walking and praying, and I distinctly sensed the Lord saying in my conscience, "This chemo is not about you. I want to get you closer to other cancer patients I want you to meet." The next day, my chemo nurse turned out to be a wonderful believer. She introduced me to three other men who had the exact diagnosis as I did. Chemo treatment centers can be unusual places. Some people want to hide; others just want to get it over with and get home. For me, the treatment center became my new congregation. Rather than hide behind curtains, we circled our chairs and began to talk. When I learned to unhook my infusion pump and let it run on batteries, I was able to meet new friends every time I went in for treatment.

I will never forget the hours after my first chemo treatment, sunk down in a chair in our living room, feeling absolutely miserable in twenty different ways. My twenty-one-year-old son came in and sat next to me. He asked, "Dad, would you teach me the Bible?" For those with children, you know how precious that moment was. He was looking at me through the eyes of an uncertain future and knew there was something I could tell him about this journey that he needed to know. In our weakest moments, God moves toward

us and asks us to extend ourselves to others.
Michael Card, in his book *A Fragile Stone*,
provides a remarkable insight from Peter's life:

*Why did Peter doubt? After all, he had
begun to accomplish it, he had walked on the
water. But there is a deeper lesson he had to
learn, and Jesus was intent on him not missing
it, even as now you and I must learn it if we
are to move forward as we walk through the
wind storm of following Jesus . . . The lesson is
that Peter needed to sink in order to take the
next step of faith in Jesus. Because walking on
water does not ultimately increase our faith, only
sinking does! Those who ask for miracles and
receive them soon forget. But those who suffer for
Christ's sake never forget. They have their own
wounds to remind them. When we are hurting,
we do not flee to the rich and healthy for wisdom
and real comfort. We seek out those who have
fellowshipped in the sufferings of Jesus.*

Contrary to popular belief, God does not place us on the sidelines of life when we walk through hardship. Rather, He takes us to the center of the playing field, so the world can watch and observe His faithfulness in our lives. This has been true throughout biblical history. Whenever God called His people into the wilderness, He always met them with His full provision. Think back to Abraham, Moses, the people of Israel, the prophets, and Jesus. They all had wilderness experiences. What is the wilderness? It is a literal place of danger and vulnerability. Where in the wilderness will we find food and water? Where will we find shelter? What about the wild animals, the bandits, and the specter of being lost? The wilderness is a real place and genuinely life-threatening. Yet over and over again, God provides for His people in their wilderness experience, *without exception*. What strength and confidence this gives us! We never enter the wilderness without His full provision of grace. This is precisely why Paul was able to say:

I have learned to be content whatever the circumstances. I know what it is to be in need, and I know what it is to have plenty. I have learned the secret of being content in any and every situation, whether well fed or hungry, whether living in plenty or in want. I can do everything through him who gives me strength. (Phil. 4:11–13)

Godly contentment is birthed out of unreserved trust. God's track record in the wilderness not only should encourage us, but also empower us to walk through the trials we face, because we are assured that God is indeed bigger than those trials.

The third witness for a follower of Jesus from our test in Hebrews is the way we die. Not long ago, Kay and I had dinner with two pastor friends and their wives. During the course of the evening, we somehow got on the topic of funeral arrangements for our deaths. We laughed as we talked about one pastor bargaining with a cemetery sales agent over buying a plot just like one would bargain for a car. Then things really got crazy when we discussed where we would spread our ashes if we were cremated. I imagine if someone were listening in, they would conclude we were a pretty sick and morose group. The truth is that we are people who have learned that finishing well in life is just as important to God as how we live our lives each day. We proved that death can, and should, have a humorous side as well. We can laugh, because we have read the final pages of the book, and we know who wins!

When we as believers talk about cancer or dying, we are really no different in our reactions than non-believers in many respects. This is most unfortunate. The real issue for Christians and non-Christians when it comes to a sickness like cancer or facing the reality of our own death is *fear*. Recently, I was speaking in a church and asked the congregation to say the word "cancer" out loud. I then asked them to say "death." You would not believe it, but less than 40 percent of the congregation could even speak out the words. You would think there was some kind of bad ju-ju by just saying it out loud, like we were drawing attention to it and we would somehow get sucked into the consequences of these words. In reflecting on the issue of fear, Rebecca Pippert says in her recent book, *A Heart For God*:

The silver lining in the dark cloud of fear is that fear pushes us to decide on our view of reality. What do I truly believe about the universe? Am I alone in this battle, or is there a God who overrules human affairs? Does my deliverance depend upon human prowess and things I can see, or does the final outcome depend on a massive resource beyond my own—the powerful, faithful, living God?[5]

All living things must die, and there is not a human being alive who does not face the issue of death and dying at some point in his or her life. Some face it early on, while others find diversions that will take them into their final hours trying to avoid the issue entirely. For the follower of Jesus, fear of death should be a non-issue. That bears repeating—our fear of death should be a non-issue. This may sound totally unrealistic for you as you struggle with the idea of dying, but when you boil it down, we are simply aligning what we claim to believe as a Christian with how we behave in daily life. How are we supposed to believe and behave regarding the issue of dying? The writer of Hebrews says it best:

Since the children have flesh and blood, he too shared in their humanity so that by his death he might destroy him who holds the power of death—that is, the devil—and free those who all their lives were <u>held in slavery by their fear of death.</u> (Heb. 2:14–15, emphasis added)

Why should we not fear death? Because
Jesus has freed us from that fear! Having been
held in slavery to this fear all of our lives,
we forget that through Jesus's death, we are,
among other things, freed from the fear of
dying. We see Jesus affirm this truth when He
looked straight into Martha's eyes, and said
in John 11:25, "I am the resurrection and
the life. He who believes in me will live, even
though he dies."

Will you allow Jesus to look you in the
eyes through your imagination and receive
this promised freedom? I want nothing more
than for Him to free you from this curse.
Once you are freed, believe me, you will know
it! You will feel like Mel Gibson in the movie
Braveheart. Gibson, playing the character of
William Wallace, had just defeated the English
in an impossible, against-all-odds battle. With
blood-spattered body, Gibson thrust his sword
into the air and gave what I consider to be the
most piercing, gut-busting, deep-soul yells of
victory I have ever witnessed. The scene is so

powerful; it brings tears to my eyes every time I watch that film. This is the true power of the gospel. It is something already given, but needs to be claimed.

Freedom from the fear of dying does interesting things to you. When I returned from New York City to Nashville after receiving my terminal cancer diagnosis, I spent the first three weeks preparing to die. As weird as this sounds, I think it is one of the greatest gifts we can give to our family in preparing for our own death. Why stick them with second guessing and arranging the details at the most tender and vulnerable time of grieving? Kay and I reviewed our financial situation and made adjustments to our wills with our financial planner and attorney. We signed over car titles and property. I contacted the funeral director and filled out all of the necessary paperwork ahead of time. I even wrote my own memorial service and distributed it to those participating in the service. Once I completed the task of preparing to die, I was totally freed up to live and to focus on the ministry God had given to me.

What are your plans for dying? Do you have anything formed in your mind yet? Personally, I am a cremation man when it comes to dealing with the remains of my body. I like the idea of a low impact exit— ashes to ashes—and the price is an incredible bargain over traditional burials. Others have strongly disagreed with me. One man came up to me after speaking in a local church one Sunday and said cremation was a pagan ritual and burial was the only biblical option. I responded by saying, "In most states, to get buried you must be embalmed. So where do you think embalming the body came from? Are you telling me the Egyptians have a distinctively Christian view of proper burial techniques?"

Before you launch a counter-defense to that remark, consider this. Why is it that we as Americans are so impatient with every aspect of life except dying? Why are we so insistent on prolonging the death process with embalming, waterproof vaults, and steel-reinforced caskets, only to come to the same state of decomposition as someone who is cremated? Certainly it cannot be because our bodies are temples of the Holy Spirit and we must revere them in death. Just look at someone in a casket for viewing in a funeral home and tell me that the one you are gazing at in death is the same person in life. The spirit of that person is not at home, and what you are looking at is the shell of a former glory. Another person insisted that God needs a body to resurrect into our new bodies. I figure that if He made me out of the dust of the earth the first time, He can do it a second time. Or is He stumped with such an assignment? Hardly. The real issue for Americans and death is control. We are so presumptuous about our mortality; we actually believe it is within our capacity to remain in control to the very end. As with life, we want death on our terms. Almost unbelievable to comprehend, but nonetheless true.

The purpose of my inquiry into these issues is not to convince you of my point of view. I am perfectly at peace with your own conscience leading you in such matters. What is important is that you not fear the process— any part of it. The only way you know you are free from the fear of death is if you can stare it in the face and not flinch. Jesus calls us, His followers, to live our lives through the eyes of eternity rather than through our mortality.

This brings us to the final verses of our text in Hebrews 12:1–2:

Therefore, since we are surrounded by such a great cloud of witnesses, let us throw off everything that hinders and the sin that so easily entangles, and let us run with perseverance the race marked out for us. Let us fix our eyes on Jesus, the author and perfecter of our faith.

God is calling us today to remember the race we are running. It is a race that stretches into eternity, and it is only run successfully when we fix our eyes in the right direction— on Jesus. God does not intend for us to face life alone. Whether we experience His miracles of deliverance, endure hardship and trials, or even face death, we remain, now and forevermore, His witnesses. This is the essence of our life in Him.

Early in the morning on February 22, 2004,

ohn finished the race and entered eternity. Later that week, friends were visiting with John's wife, Kay. Among us were Rwandan friends that John mentioned in several of his emails. Aster Rutibabalira asked Kay about the specific time John had died. Kay explained that it was some time between 3:30 and 4:00 AM on Sunday morning.

Aster went on to explain why he was so interested in the actual time of John's death. Here is my paraphrase of what he shared with Kay:

One of John's friends woke up suddenly, around 4:00 Sunday morning. As she often did, she immediately thought of John and began praying for him. As usual, she started to ask Jesus to heal John. But as she started to pray, she stopped, and sensed in her spirit that she no longer needed to pray, "Jesus, please heal our friend John." John was no longer with us. So she started to pray, "Jesus, look for our friend John."

While all of us who knew and loved John ache with the reality of his loss, we celebrate the reality voiced by our Rwandan friend— our friend John is with Jesus. We will see him again.

Death is real but it is not final. We imagine John walking toward Jesus's throne, joined by a crowd of faithful followers who comprised the group of "first-timers" that Sunday morning. We picture John's huge smile as he walks to Jesus and waits for his face-to-face encounter. And we celebrate with John the affirmation Jesus gives our friend, "Well done, faithful servant. You finished well."

NOTES

1. Pippert, Rebecca. *A Heart for God* (Downers Grove, IL: Intervarsity, 1996), 28–29.
2. Card, Michael. *A Fragile Stone* (Downers Grove, IL: Intervarsity, 2003), 53.
3. McGill, Arthur. *Suffering: A Test of Theological Method* (Philadelphia: Westminster, 1982), 55.
4. Card, Michael. *A Fragile Stone* (Downers Grove, IL: Intervarsity, 2003), 53.
5. Pippert, Rebecca. *A Heart for God* (Downers Grove, IL: Intervarsity, 1996), 28–29.